TRACK PLANS
FOR TOY TRAINS

KALMBACH
BOOKS

INTRODUCTION

This book includes O and S gauge track plans that offer endless possibilities for creating your ideal layout. They range from simple ovals that can be quickly assembled on the floor or on a small table to large, complex configurations that require numerous track sections and a fair amount of permanently available space.

For each track plan you'll find gridline measurements in inches or feet that indicate the dimensions of the layout. You'll also find a track list that shows the suggested quantity and type of track you can use to assemble the layout. Bear in mind that a number of different manufacturers offer a wide variety of track components, so you'll want to closely examine the plan you select to see how each track section works to form the layout. Of course, new track products continue to be introduced, so you'll also want to check with your local hobby shop and read *Classic Toy Trains* magazine to keep informed of any new releases from the manufacturers listed at the back of this book.

Printed in the United States of America

02 03 04 05 06 07 08   10 9 8 7 6 5 4 3 2

Visit our website at
http://kalmbachbooks.com
Secure online ordering available

Publisher's Cataloging in Publication
(Provided by Quality Books, Inc.)

Track plans for toy trains. — 1st ed.
    p. cm.
    ISBN: 0-89778-444-8

    1. Railroads—Models. 2. Railroads—Track.

TF197.T73 1999   625.1'9
                    QBI99-10

Book design: Denise Folger
Cover design: Kristi Ludwig

The plans in this book were rendered using RR-Track® computer design software by R&S Enterprises, Jonestown, Pennsylvania.

CONTENTS

CHAPTER ONE
Track Plans for Small O Gauge Layouts

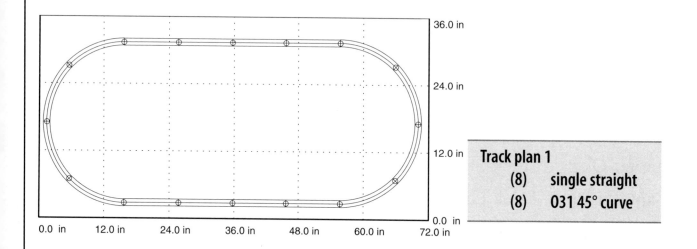

Track plan 1
- (8)   single straight
- (8)   031 45° curve

Track plan 2
- (10)   single straight
- (16)   031 45° curve

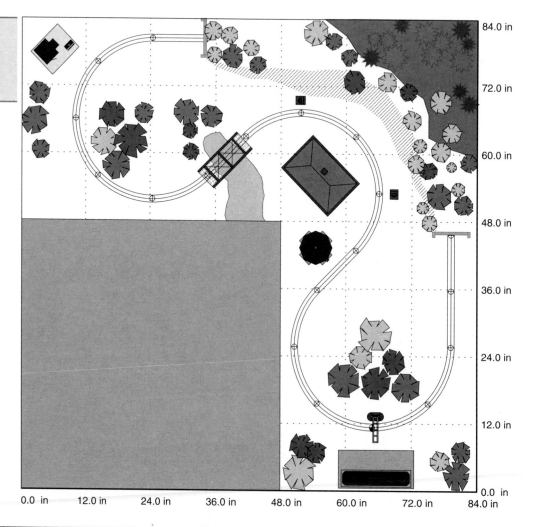

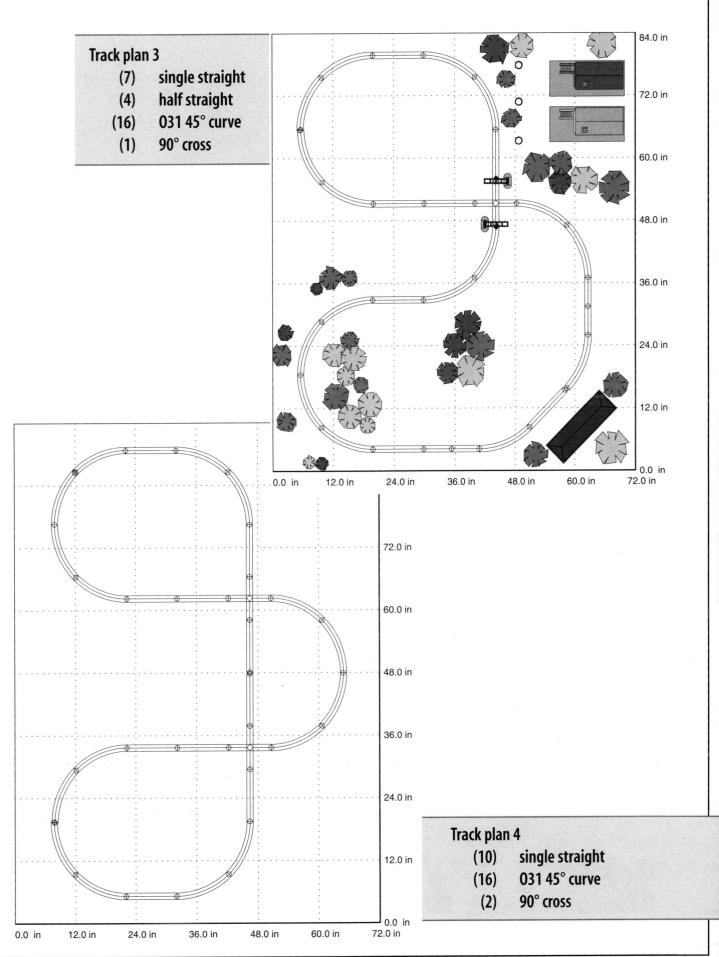

Track plan 3

(7)	single straight
(4)	half straight
(16)	031 45° curve
(1)	90° cross

Track plan 4

(10)	single straight
(16)	031 45° curve
(2)	90° cross

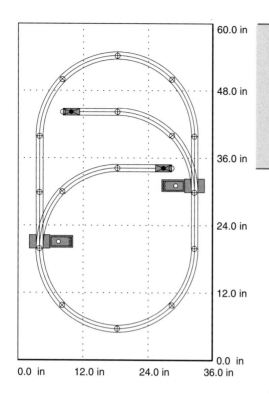

Track plan 5

(4)	single straight
(10)	031 45° curve
(1)	031 left-hand turnout
(1)	031 right-hand turnout
(2)	track bumper

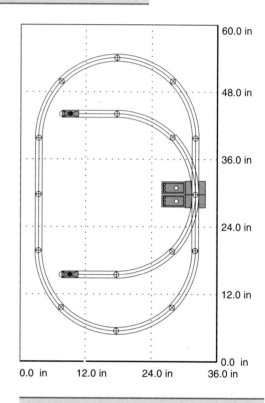

Track plan 6

(4)	single straight
(10)	031 45° curve
(1)	031 left-hand turnout
(1)	031 right-hand turnout
(2)	track bumper

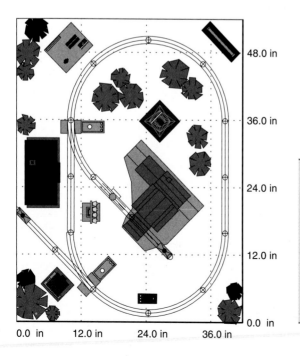

Track plan 7

(5)	single straight
(7)	031 45° curve
(1)	031 left-hand turnout
(1)	031 right-hand turnout
(1)	uncoupling track
(2)	track bumper

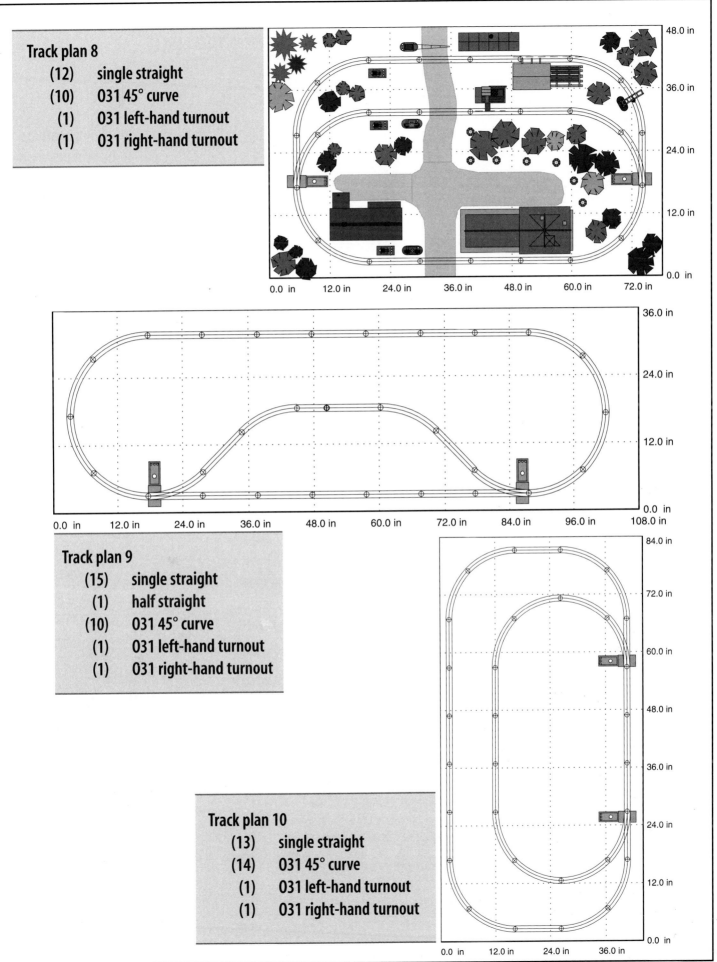

Track plan 8
- (12)　single straight
- (10)　031 45° curve
- (1)　031 left-hand turnout
- (1)　031 right-hand turnout

Track plan 9
- (15)　single straight
- (1)　half straight
- (10)　031 45° curve
- (1)　031 left-hand turnout
- (1)　031 right-hand turnout

Track plan 10
- (13)　single straight
- (14)　031 45° curve
- (1)　031 left-hand turnout
- (1)　031 right-hand turnout

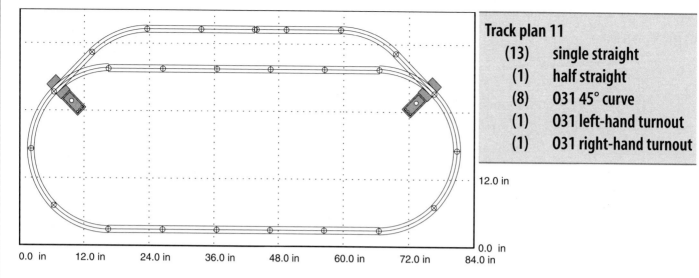

Track plan 11

(13)	single straight
(1)	half straight
(8)	031 45° curve
(1)	031 left-hand turnout
(1)	031 right-hand turnout

Track plan 12

(16)	single straight
(2)	half straight
(8)	031 45° curve
(2)	031 left-hand turnout
(2)	031 right-hand turnout

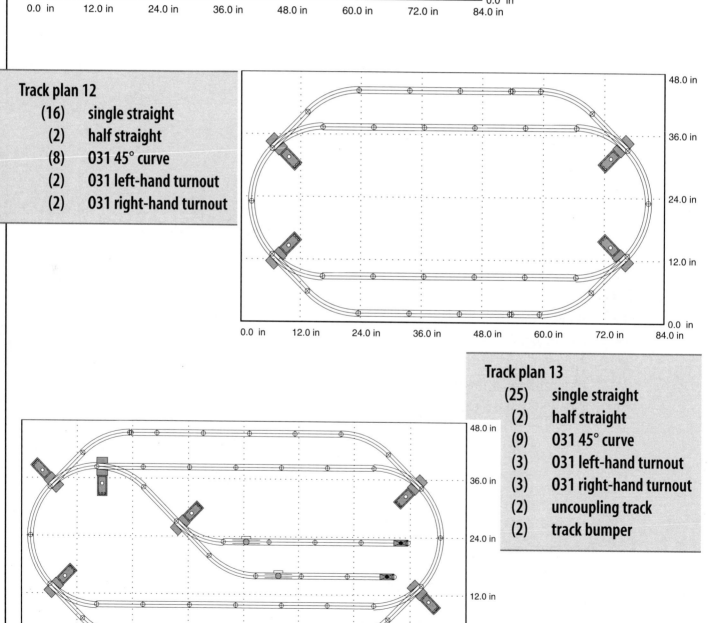

Track plan 13

(25)	single straight
(2)	half straight
(9)	031 45° curve
(3)	031 left-hand turnout
(3)	031 right-hand turnout
(2)	uncoupling track
(2)	track bumper

Track plan 14

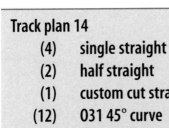

(4)	single straight
(2)	half straight
(1)	custom cut straight
(12)	031 45° curve
(1)	031 left-hand turnout
(1)	031 right-hand turnout
(1)	90° cross

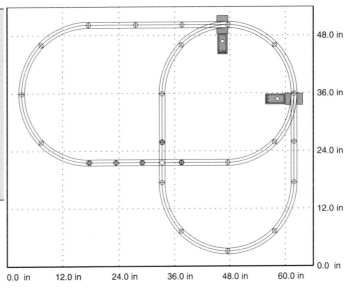

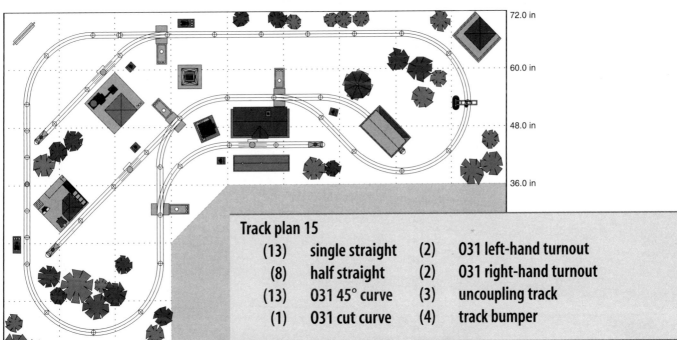

Track plan 15

(13)	single straight	(2)	031 left-hand turnout
(8)	half straight	(2)	031 right-hand turnout
(13)	031 45° curve	(3)	uncoupling track
(1)	031 cut curve	(4)	track bumper

Track plan 16

(10)	single straight
(3)	half straight
(1)	custom cut straight
(14)	031 45° curve
(1)	031 left-hand turnout
(1)	031 right-hand turnout
(1)	90° cross

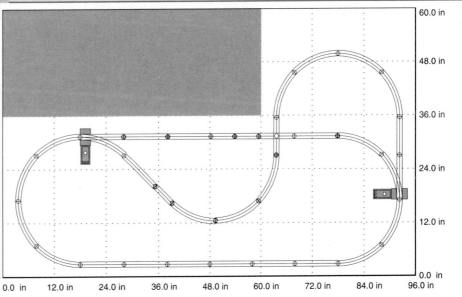

Track plan 17

- (12)   single straight
- (10)   031 45° curve
- (2)   031 left-hand turnout
- (2)   031 right-hand turnout
- (4)   uncoupling track
- (4)   track bumper

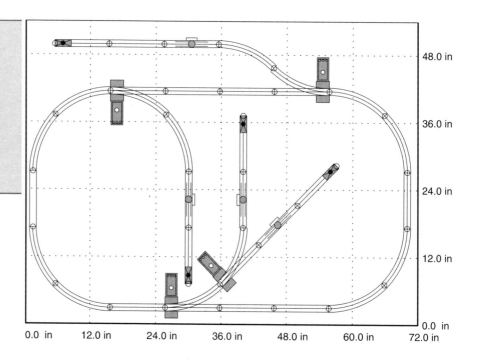

Track plan 18

(25)	single straight	(2)	uncoupling track
(5)	half straight	(1)	022 right-hand turnout
(2)	custom cut straight	(2)	031 left-hand turnout
(10)	031 45° curve	(1)	031 right-hand turnout
(1)	022 makeup curve	(2)	track bumper

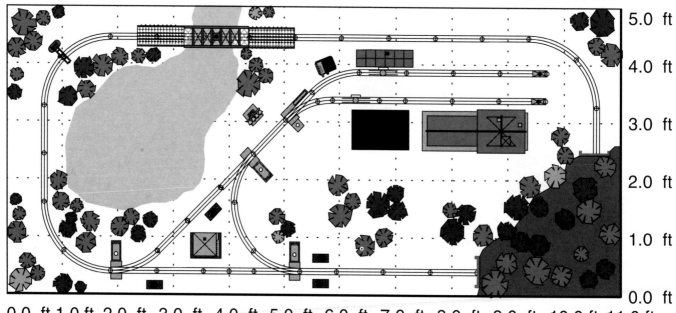

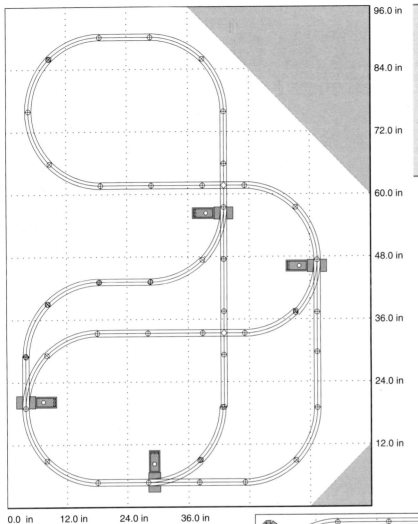

Track plan 19

(9)	single straight
(4)	custom cut straight
(18)	031 45° curve
(1)	031 left-hand turnout
(3)	031 right-hand turnout
(2)	90° cross

96.0 in
84.0 in
72.0 in
60.0 in
48.0 in
36.0 in
24.0 in
12.0 in

0.0 in   12.0 in   24.0 in   36.0 in

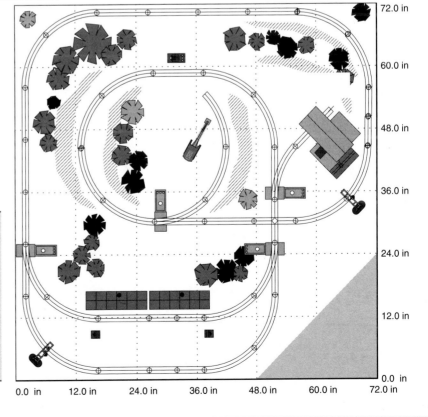

Track plan 20

(12)	single straight
(6)	half straight
(20)	031 45° curve
(2)	031 left-hand turnout
(2)	031 right-hand turnout
(1)	90° cross

72.0 in
60.0 in
48.0 in
36.0 in
24.0 in
12.0 in
0.0 in

0.0 in   12.0 in   24.0 in   36.0 in   48.0 in   60.0 in   72.0 in

CHAPTER TWO
Track Plans for Small S Gauge Layouts

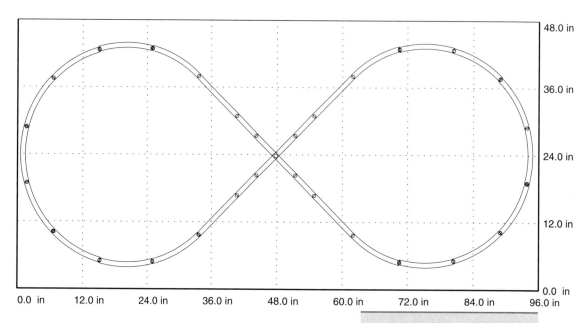

48.0 in
36.0 in
24.0 in
12.0 in
0.0 in

0.0 in 12.0 in 24.0 in 36.0 in 48.0 in 60.0 in 72.0 in 84.0 in 96.0 in

Track plan 21
- (4) single straight
- (4) half straight
- (18) S-40 curve
- (1) 90° cross

Track plan 22
- (8) single straight
- (16) S-40 curve
- (1) remote left-hand turnout
- (1) remote right-hand turnout

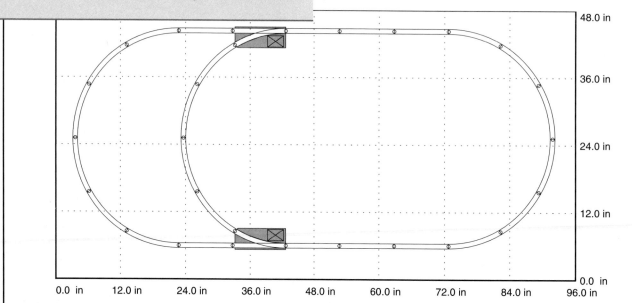

48.0 in
36.0 in
24.0 in
12.0 in
0.0 in

0.0 in 12.0 in 24.0 in 36.0 in 48.0 in 60.0 in 72.0 in 84.0 in 96.0 in

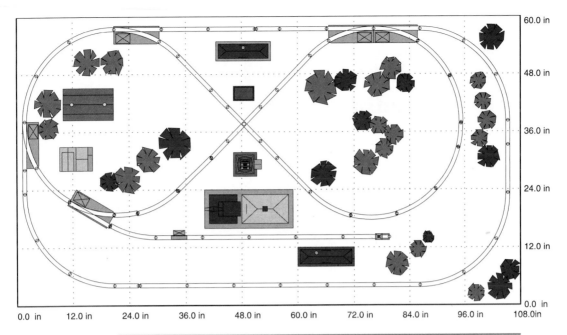

60.0 in
48.0 in
36.0 in
24.0 in
12.0 in
0.0 in

0.0 in 12.0 in 24.0 in 36.0 in 48.0 in 60.0 in 72.0 in 84.0 in 96.0 in 108.0in

Track plan 23

(18)	straight	(2)	remote right-hand turnout
(8)	half straight	(1)	90° cross
(21)	S-40 curve	(1)	uncoupling track
(4)	S-40 half curve	(1)	lighted bumper
(3)	remote left-hand turnout		

Track plan 24

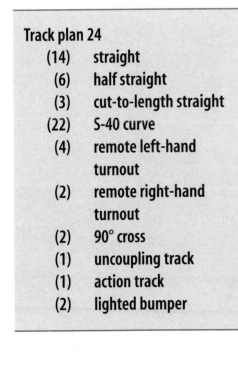

(14) straight
(6) half straight
(3) cut-to-length straight
(22) S-40 curve
(4) remote left-hand turnout
(2) remote right-hand turnout
(2) 90° cross
(1) uncoupling track
(1) action track
(2) lighted bumper

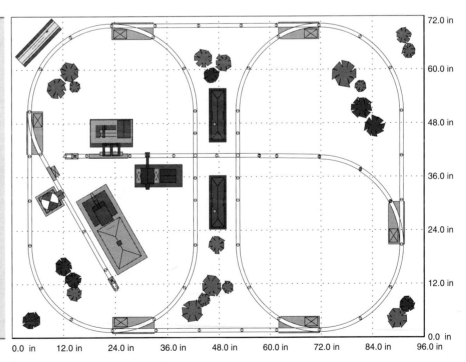

72.0 in
60.0 in
48.0 in
36.0 in
24.0 in
12.0 in
0.0 in

0.0 in 12.0 in 24.0 in 36.0 in 48.0 in 60.0 in 72.0 in 84.0 in 96.0 in

CHAPTER THREE
Track Plans for Medium-Sized O Gauge Layouts

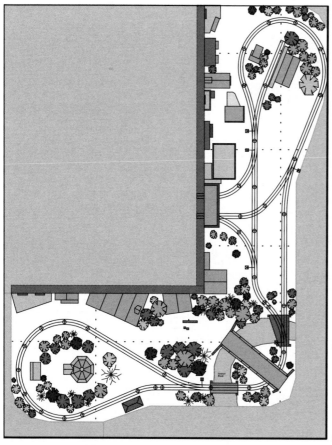

96.0 in

72.0 in

48.0 in

24.0 in

0.0 in

0.0 in   24.0 in   48.0 in   72.0 in

Track plan 25

(10)	GarGraves cut straight
(19)	GarGraves custom bent curve
(2)	Ross 031 45° left-hand switch
(2)	Ross 031 45° right-hand switch
(1)	Ross 042 30° right-hand switch
(2)	Ross 072 ±22.5° "Y" switch

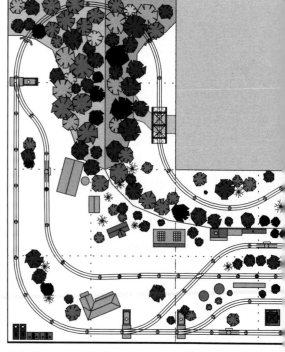

0.0 ft   2.0 ft   4.0 ft   6.0 ft

Track plan 26

(17)	single straight	(4)	031 left-hand turnout
(19)	half straight	(1)	031 right-hand turnout
(6)	031 45° curve	(1)	45° cross
(20)	042 30° curve	(4)	uncoupling track
(1)	054 curve	(1)	track bumper

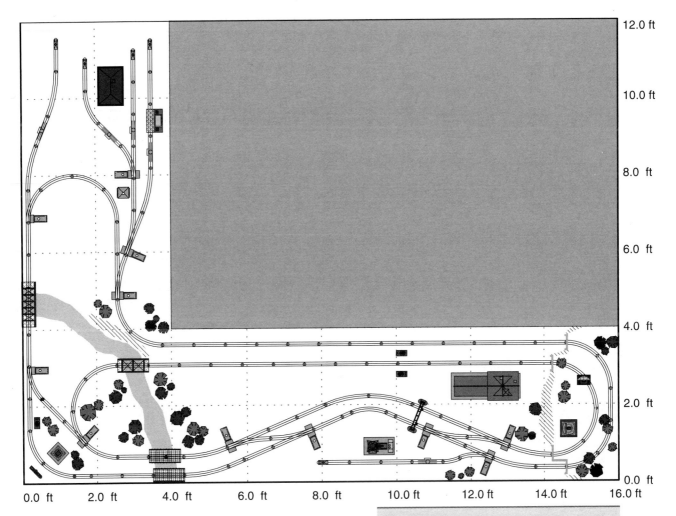

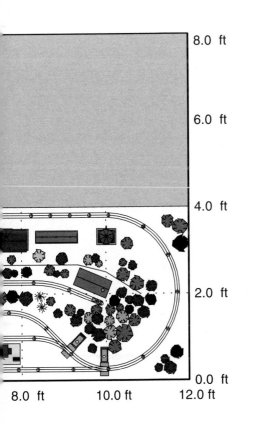

Track plan 27

- (58) single straight
- (5) half straight
- (2) custom cut straight
- (19) 031 45° curve
- (1) 031 22.5° half curve
- (1) 031 cut curve
- (9) 072 22.5° curve
- (3) 031 left-hand turnout
- (2) 031 right-hand turnout
- (3) 072 left-hand turnout
- (3) 072 right-hand turnout
- (5) uncoupling track
- (5) track bumper

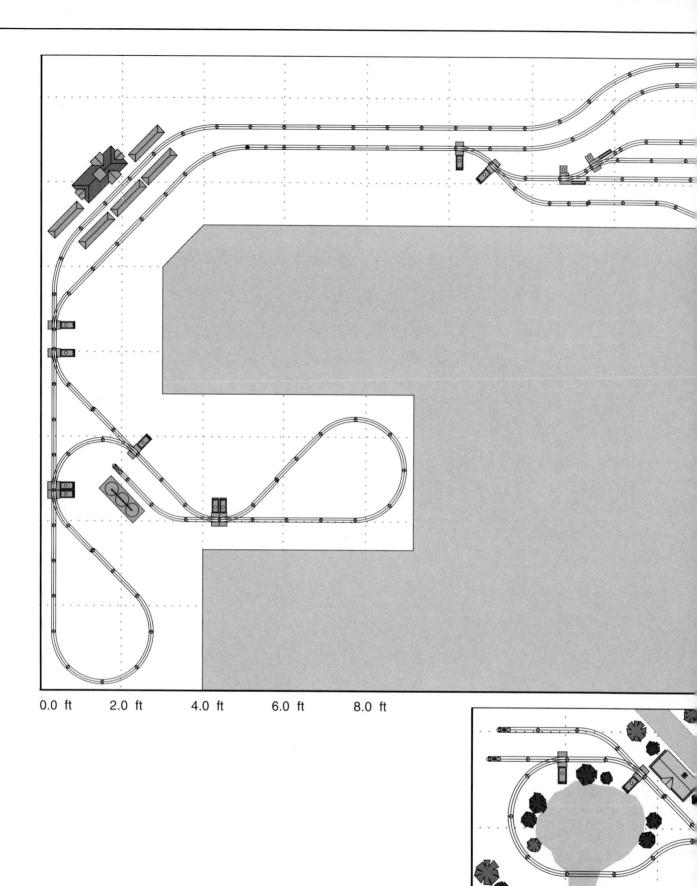

0.0 ft   2.0 ft   4.0 ft   6.0 ft   8.0 ft

0.0 ft   2.0 ft   4.0 ft

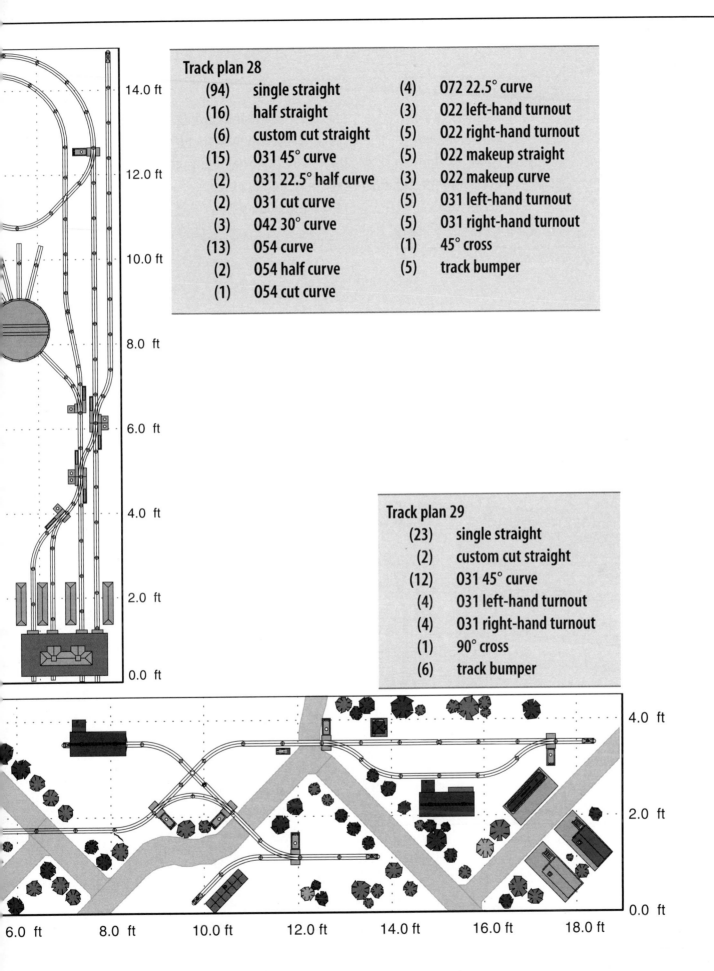

Track plan 28

(94)	single straight
(16)	half straight
(6)	custom cut straight
(15)	031 45° curve
(2)	031 22.5° half curve
(2)	031 cut curve
(3)	042 30° curve
(13)	054 curve
(2)	054 half curve
(1)	054 cut curve
(4)	072 22.5° curve
(3)	022 left-hand turnout
(5)	022 right-hand turnout
(5)	022 makeup straight
(3)	022 makeup curve
(5)	031 left-hand turnout
(5)	031 right-hand turnout
(1)	45° cross
(5)	track bumper

Track plan 29

(23)	single straight
(2)	custom cut straight
(12)	031 45° curve
(4)	031 left-hand turnout
(4)	031 right-hand turnout
(1)	90° cross
(6)	track bumper

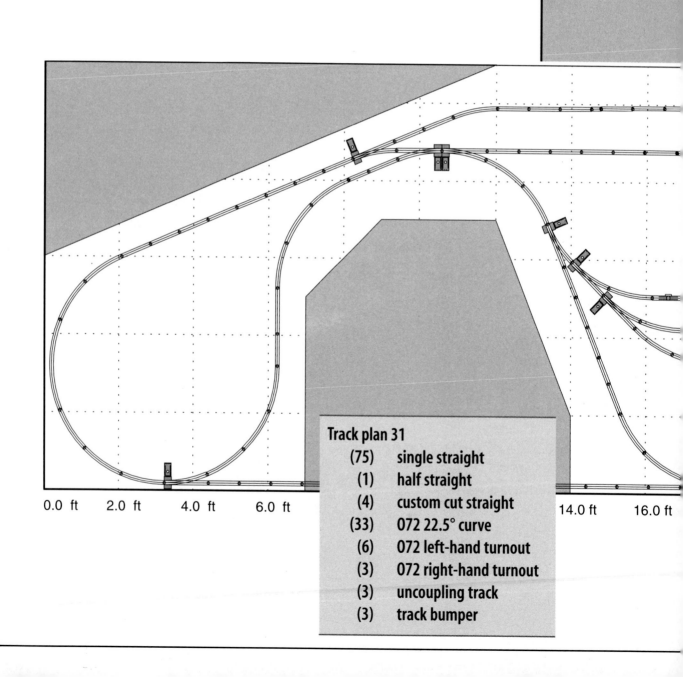

Track plan 30

(139)	single straight	(2)	031 left-hand turnout
(9)	half straight	(3)	072 left-hand turnout
(11)	40" straight	(8)	072 right-hand turnout
(1)	custom cut straight	(5)	uncoupling track
(1)	054 curve	(4)	track bumper
(39)	072 22.5° curve		

Track plan 31

(75)	single straight
(1)	half straight
(4)	custom cut straight
(33)	072 22.5° curve
(6)	072 left-hand turnout
(3)	072 right-hand turnout
(3)	uncoupling track
(3)	track bumper

0.0 ft   2.0 ft   4.0 ft   6.0 ft   14.0 ft   16.0 ft

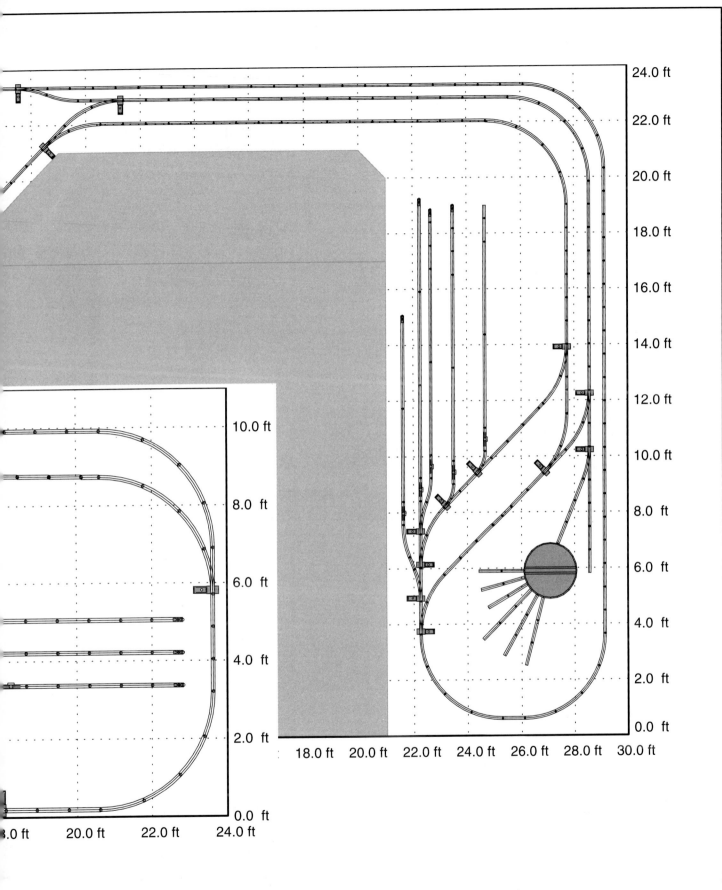

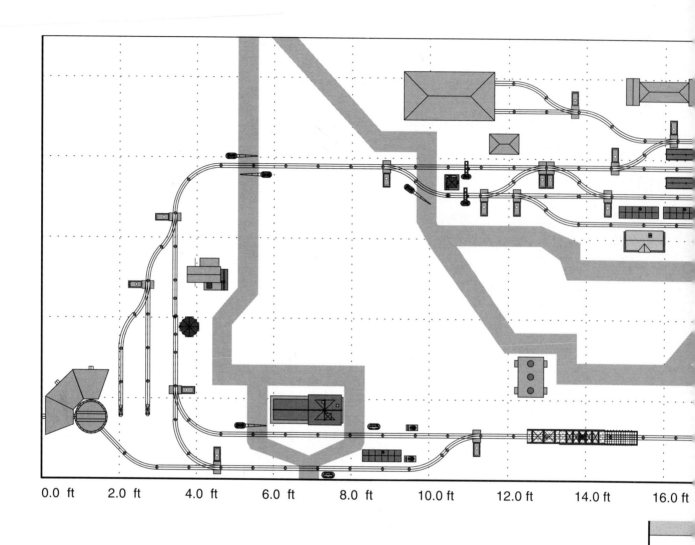

0.0 ft   2.0 ft   4.0 ft   6.0 ft   8.0 ft   10.0 ft   12.0 ft   14.0 ft   16.0 ft

Track plan 33

(63)	single straight	(1)	054 cut curve
(5)	half straight	(6)	072 left-hand turnout
(4)	custom cut straight	(2)	072 right-hand turnout
(50)	054 curve	(4)	uncoupling track
(3)	054 half curve	(6)	track bumper

0.0 ft

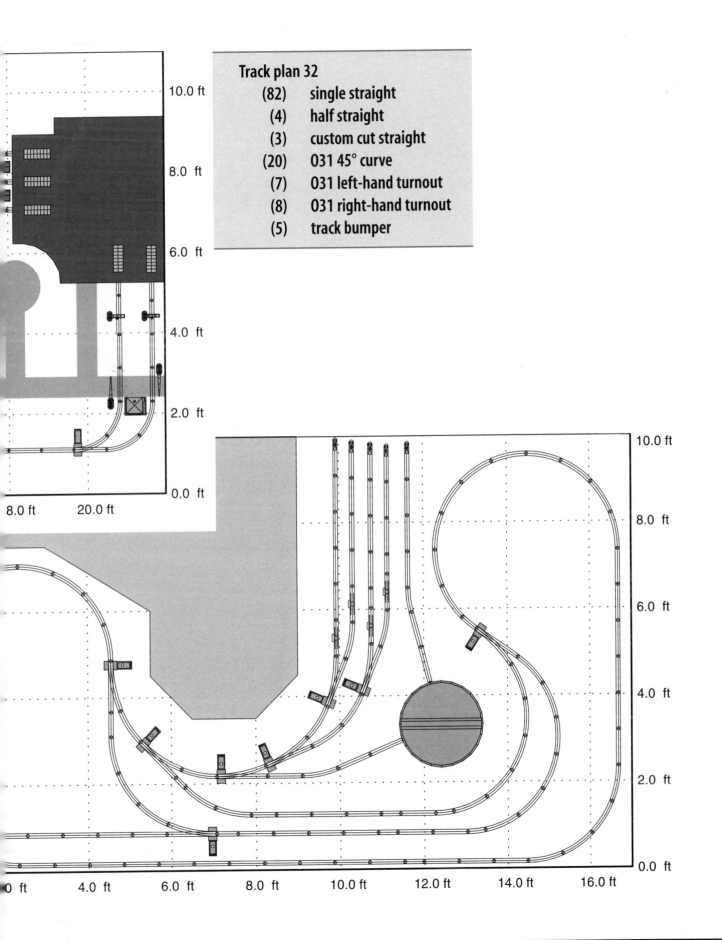

Track plan 32

- (82) single straight
- (4) half straight
- (3) custom cut straight
- (20) 031 45° curve
- (7) 031 left-hand turnout
- (8) 031 right-hand turnout
- (5) track bumper

10.0 ft

8.0 ft

6.0 ft

4.0 ft

2.0 ft

0.0 ft

8.0 ft   20.0 ft

10.0 ft

8.0 ft

6.0 ft

4.0 ft

2.0 ft

0.0 ft

0 ft   4.0 ft   6.0 ft   8.0 ft   10.0 ft   12.0 ft   14.0 ft   16.0 ft

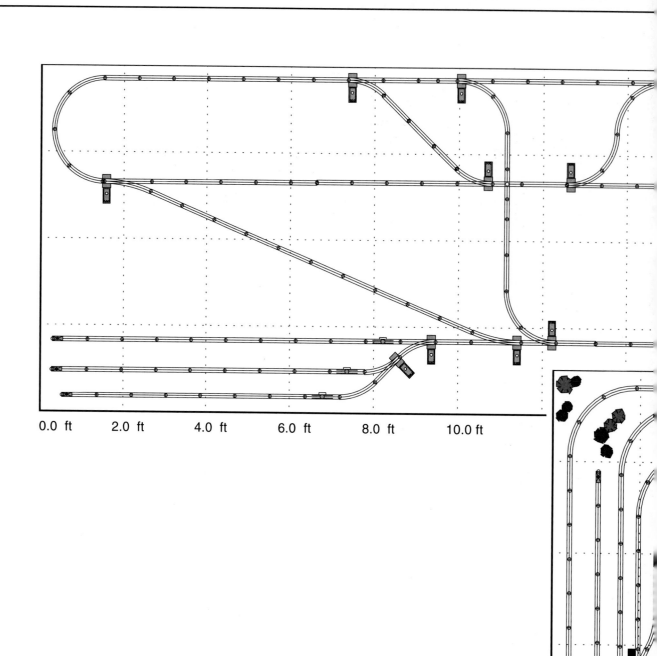

0.0 ft   2.0 ft   4.0 ft   6.0 ft   8.0 ft   10.0 ft

Track plan 35

(162)	Super O straight
(5)	Super O half straight
(5)	Super O cut-to-length straight
(48)	Super O 036 curve
(14)	Super O 036 half curve
(5)	Super O manual left-hand turnout
(5)	Super O manual right-hand turnout
(8)	track bumper

0.0 ft   2.0 ft

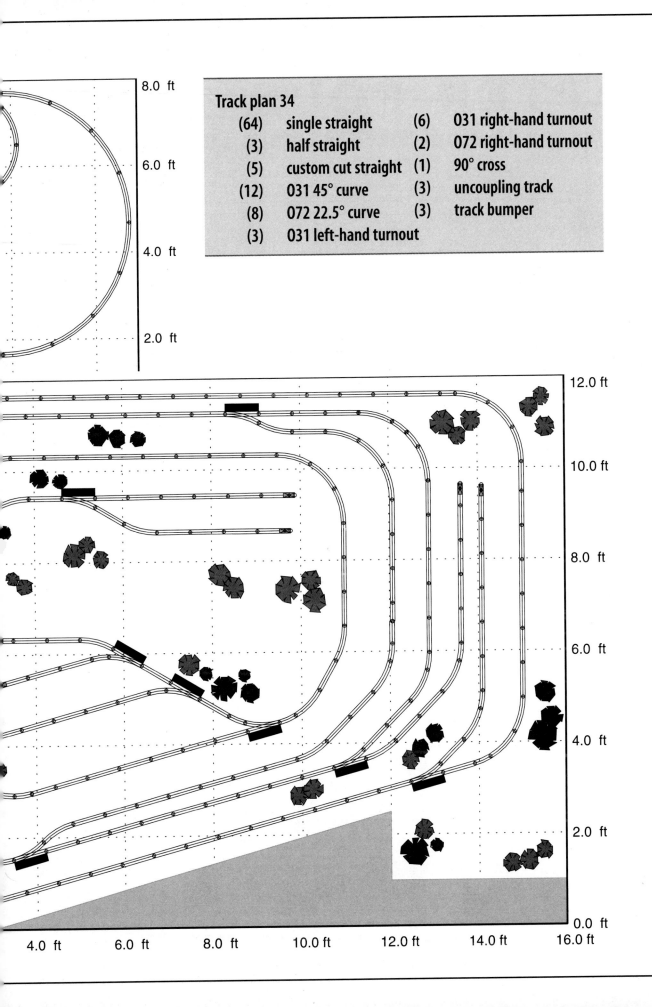

Track plan 34

(64)	single straight	(6)	031 right-hand turnout
(3)	half straight	(2)	072 right-hand turnout
(5)	custom cut straight	(1)	90° cross
(12)	031 45° curve	(3)	uncoupling track
(8)	072 22.5° curve	(3)	track bumper
(3)	031 left-hand turnout		

CHAPTER FOUR
Track Plans for Medium-Sized S Gauge Layouts

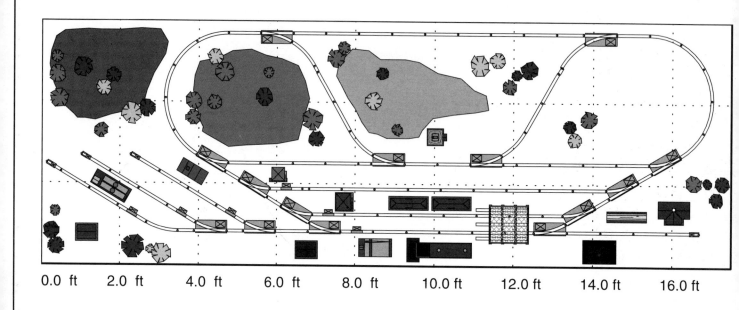

0.0 ft   2.0 ft   4.0 ft   6.0 ft   8.0 ft   10.0 ft   12.0 ft   14.0 ft   16.0 ft

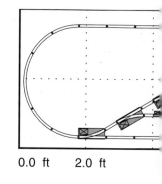

0.0 ft   2.0 ft

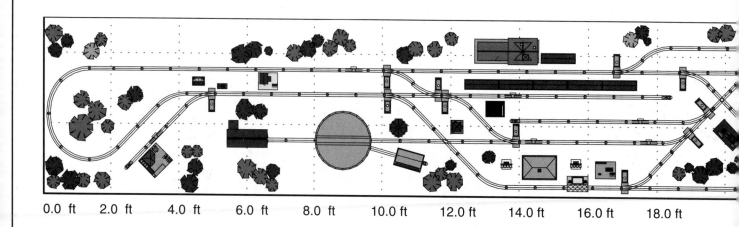

0.0 ft   2.0 ft   4.0 ft   6.0 ft   8.0 ft   10.0 ft   12.0 ft   14.0 ft   16.0 ft   18.0 ft

Track plan 36

(56)	straight
(7)	half straight
(8)	custom cut straight
(15)	S-40 curve
(6)	remote left-hand turnout
(8)	remote right-hand turnout
(6)	uncoupling track
(4)	lighted bumper

Track plan 37

(96)	straight
(12)	half straight
(4)	custom cut straight
(12)	S-40 curve
(6)	remote left-hand turnout
(6)	remote right-hand turnout
(7)	uncoupling track

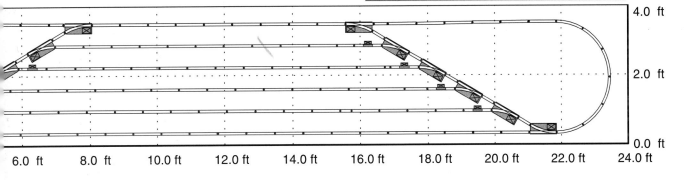

4.0 ft

2.0 ft

0.0 ft

6.0 ft   8.0 ft   10.0 ft   12.0 ft   14.0 ft   16.0 ft   18.0 ft   20.0 ft   22.0 ft   24.0 ft

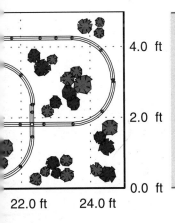

4.0 ft

2.0 ft

0.0 ft

22.0 ft   24.0 ft

Track plan 38

(65)	single straight	(8)	031 right-hand turnout
(5)	half straight	(1)	45° cross
(9)	custom cut straight	(2)	90° cross
(17)	031 45° curve	(6)	uncoupling track
(4)	031 left-hand turnout	(5)	track bumper

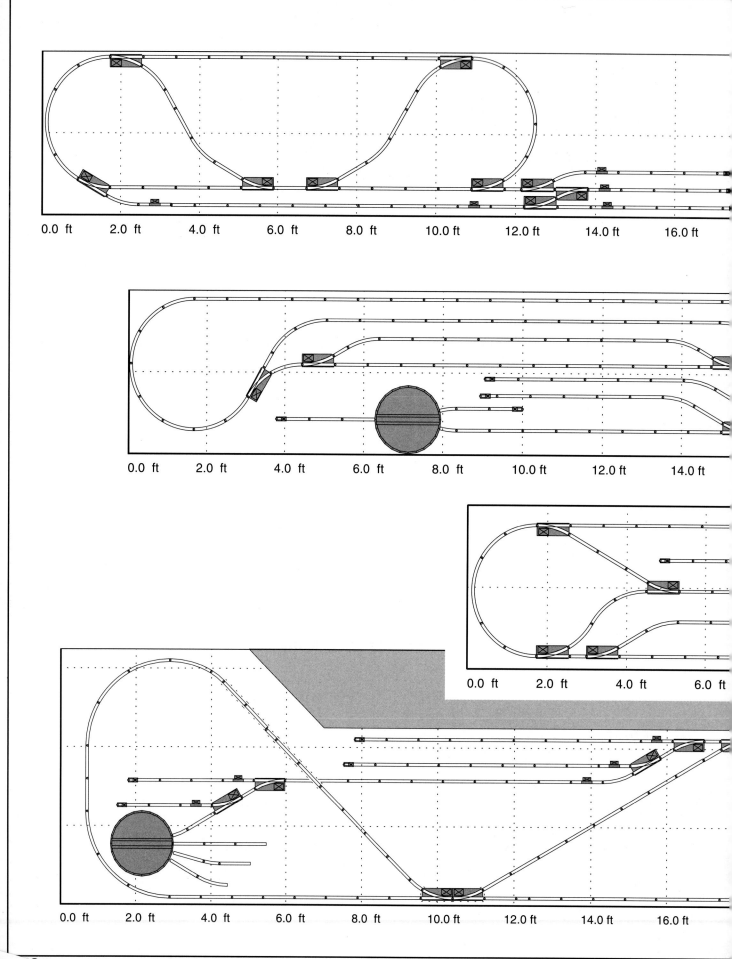

0.0 ft   2.0 ft   4.0 ft   6.0 ft   8.0 ft   10.0 ft   12.0 ft   14.0 ft   16.0 ft

0.0 ft   2.0 ft   4.0 ft   6.0 ft   8.0 ft   10.0 ft   12.0 ft   14.0 ft

0.0 ft   2.0 ft   4.0 ft   6.0 ft

0.0 ft   2.0 ft   4.0 ft   6.0 ft   8.0 ft   10.0 ft   12.0 ft   14.0 ft   16.0 ft

Track plan 39

(41)	straight	(7)	remote left-hand turnout
(4)	half straight	(2)	remote right-hand turnout
(3)	custom cut straight	(5)	uncoupling track
(16)	S-40 curve	(3)	lighted bumper

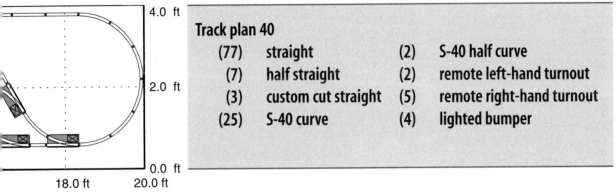

Track plan 40

(77)	straight	(2)	S-40 half curve
(7)	half straight	(2)	remote left-hand turnout
(3)	custom cut straight	(5)	remote right-hand turnout
(25)	S-40 curve	(4)	lighted bumper

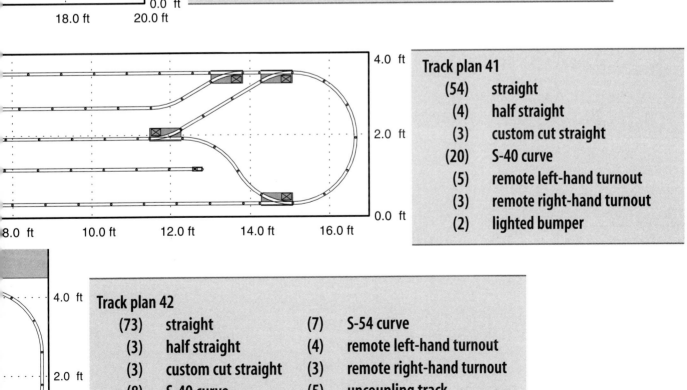

Track plan 41

(54)	straight
(4)	half straight
(3)	custom cut straight
(20)	S-40 curve
(5)	remote left-hand turnout
(3)	remote right-hand turnout
(2)	lighted bumper

Track plan 42

(73)	straight	(7)	S-54 curve
(3)	half straight	(4)	remote left-hand turnout
(3)	custom cut straight	(3)	remote right-hand turnout
(8)	S-40 curve	(5)	uncoupling track
(4)	S-40 half curve	(4)	lighted bumper

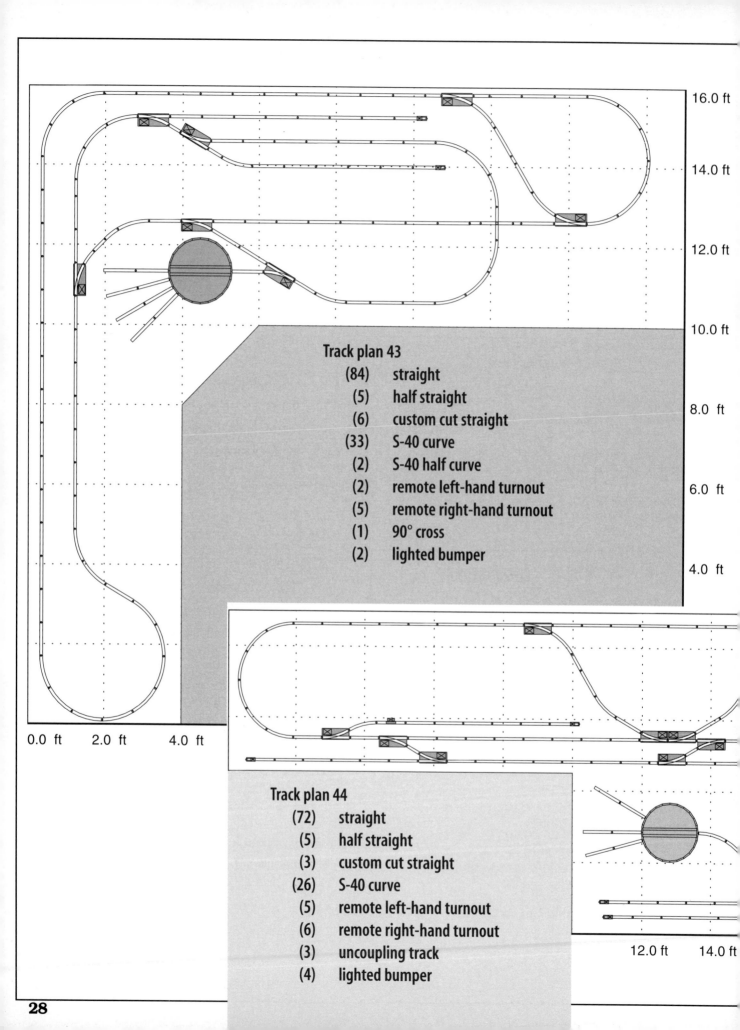

Track plan 43

(84)	straight
(5)	half straight
(6)	custom cut straight
(33)	S-40 curve
(2)	S-40 half curve
(2)	remote left-hand turnout
(5)	remote right-hand turnout
(1)	90° cross
(2)	lighted bumper

16.0 ft

14.0 ft

12.0 ft

10.0 ft

8.0 ft

6.0 ft

4.0 ft

0.0 ft   2.0 ft   4.0 ft

Track plan 44

(72)	straight
(5)	half straight
(3)	custom cut straight
(26)	S-40 curve
(5)	remote left-hand turnout
(6)	remote right-hand turnout
(3)	uncoupling track
(4)	lighted bumper

12.0 ft   14.0 ft

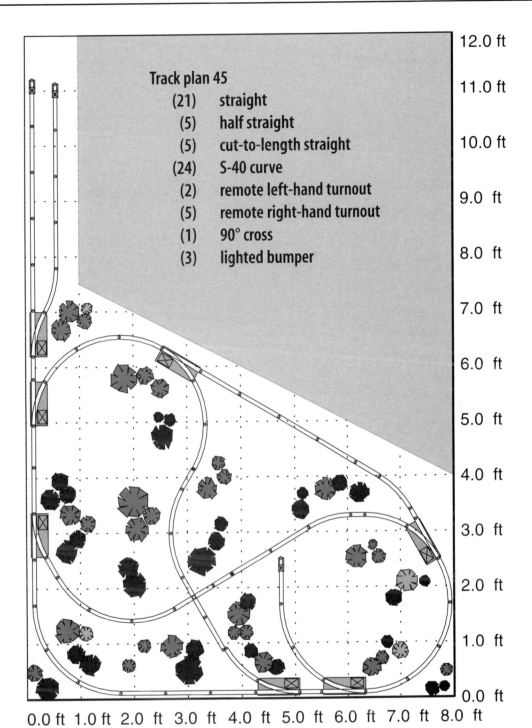

Track plan 45

(21)	straight
(5)	half straight
(5)	cut-to-length straight
(24)	S-40 curve
(2)	remote left-hand turnout
(5)	remote right-hand turnout
(1)	90° cross
(3)	lighted bumper

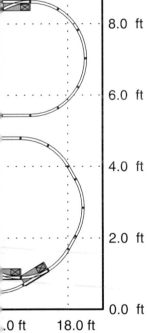

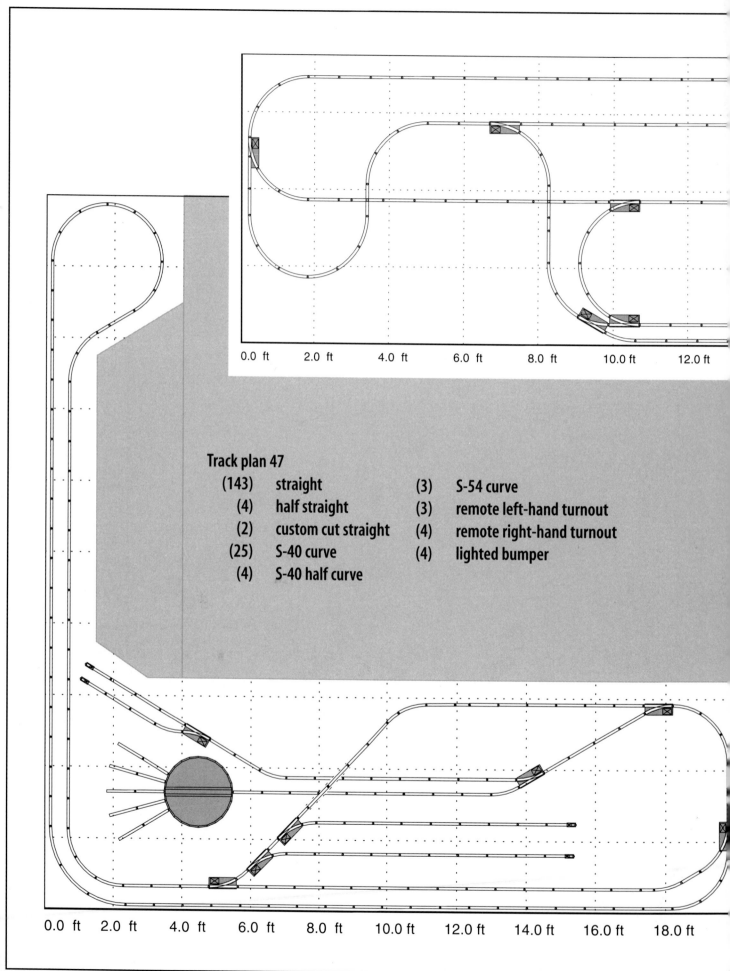

Track plan 47
- (143) straight
- (4) half straight
- (2) custom cut straight
- (25) S-40 curve
- (4) S-40 half curve
- (3) S-54 curve
- (3) remote left-hand turnout
- (4) remote right-hand turnout
- (4) lighted bumper

0.0 ft 2.0 ft 4.0 ft 6.0 ft 8.0 ft 10.0 ft 12.0 ft

0.0 ft 2.0 ft 4.0 ft 6.0 ft 8.0 ft 10.0 ft 12.0 ft 14.0 ft 16.0 ft 18.0 ft

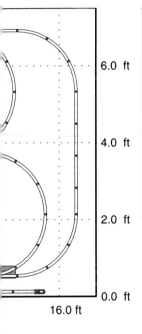

6.0 ft

4.0 ft

2.0 ft

0.0 ft

16.0 ft

Track plan 46

(47)	straight
(7)	custom cut straight
(38)	S-40 curve
(5)	remote left-hand turnout
(3)	remote right-hand turnout
(2)	90° cross
(2)	lighted bumper

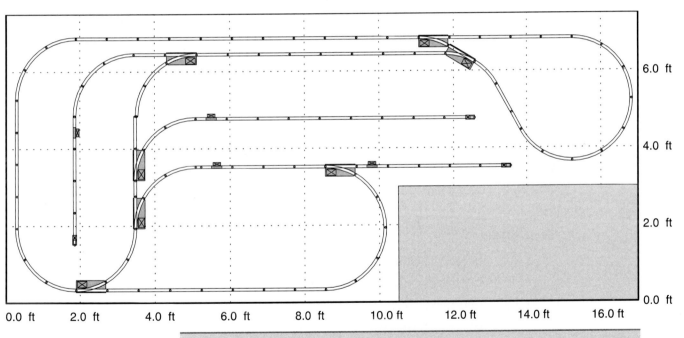

6.0 ft

4.0 ft

2.0 ft

0.0 ft

0.0 ft   2.0 ft   4.0 ft   6.0 ft   8.0 ft   10.0 ft   12.0 ft   14.0 ft   16.0 ft

Track plan 48

(55)	straight	(3)	remote left-hand turnout
(1)	half straight	(4)	remote right-hand turnout
(2)	custom cut straight	(4)	uncoupling track
(31)	S-40 curve	(3)	lighted bumper

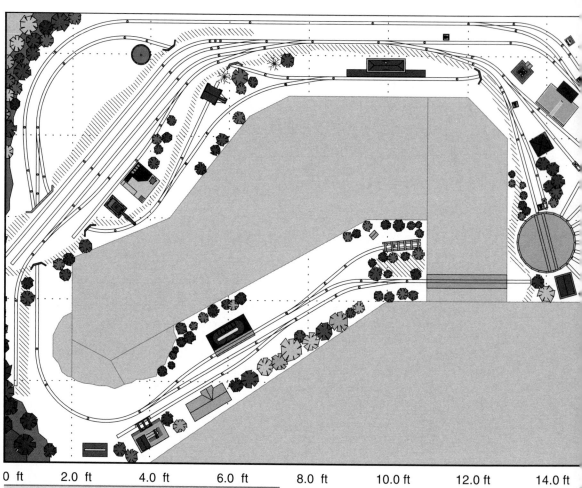

0 ft   2.0 ft   4.0 ft   6.0 ft   8.0 ft   10.0 ft   12.0 ft   14.0 ft

Track plan 49

(12)	GarGraves straight
(34)	GarGraves custom cut straight
(14)	GarGraves curve
(12)	custom cut curve
(6)	S-42 GarGraves curve
(2)	S-54 GarGraves curve
(2)	S-63 GarGraves curve
(1)	S-72 GarGraves curve
(14)	left-hand GarGraves turnout
(5)	right-hand GarGraves turnout
(10)	lighted bumper

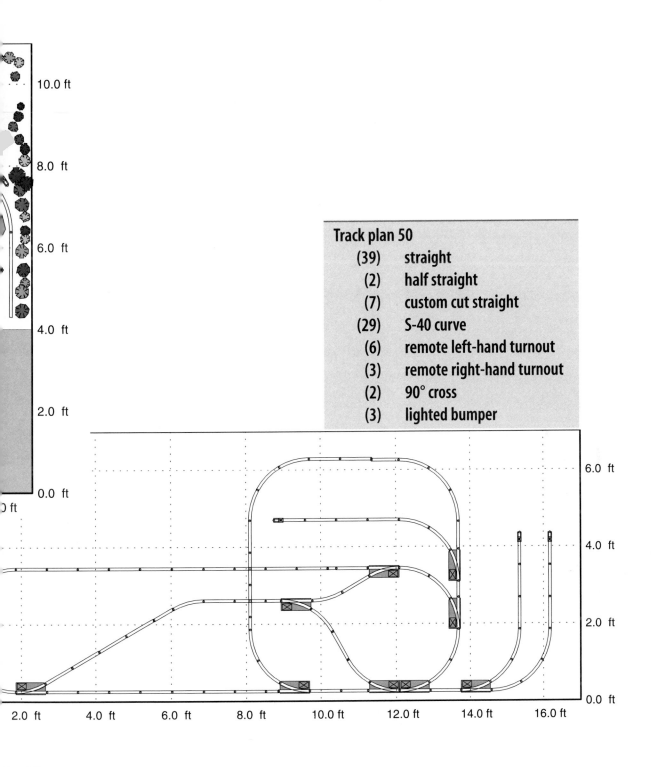

Track plan 50

(39)	straight
(2)	half straight
(7)	custom cut straight
(29)	S-40 curve
(6)	remote left-hand turnout
(3)	remote right-hand turnout
(2)	90° cross
(3)	lighted bumper

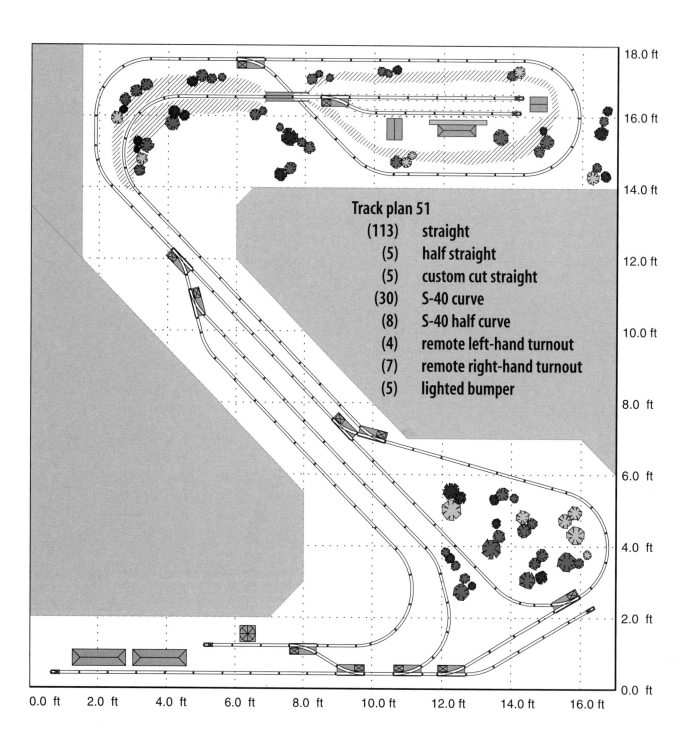

18.0 ft

16.0 ft

Track plan 51
- (113)   straight
- (5)   half straight
- (5)   custom cut straight
- (30)   S-40 curve
- (8)   S-40 half curve
- (4)   remote left-hand turnout
- (7)   remote right-hand turnout
- (5)   lighted bumper

14.0 ft

12.0 ft

10.0 ft

8.0 ft

6.0 ft

4.0 ft

2.0 ft

0.0 ft

0.0 ft   2.0 ft   4.0 ft   6.0 ft   8.0 ft   10.0 ft   12.0 ft   14.0 ft   16.0 ft

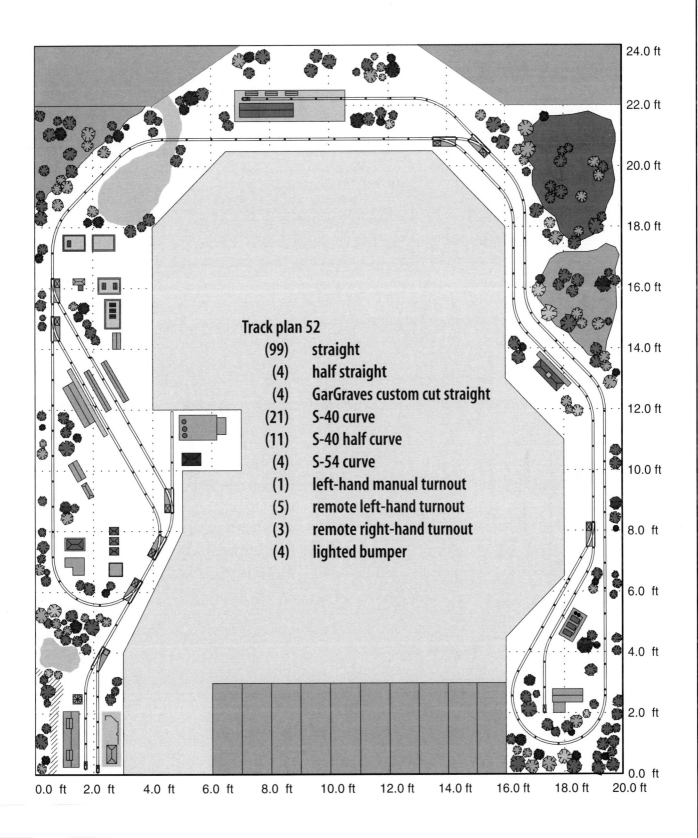

Track plan 52
- (99)   straight
- (4)   half straight
- (4)   GarGraves custom cut straight
- (21)   S-40 curve
- (11)   S-40 half curve
- (4)   S-54 curve
- (1)   left-hand manual turnout
- (5)   remote left-hand turnout
- (3)   remote right-hand turnout
- (4)   lighted bumper

CHAPTER FIVE
Track Plans for Large Layouts

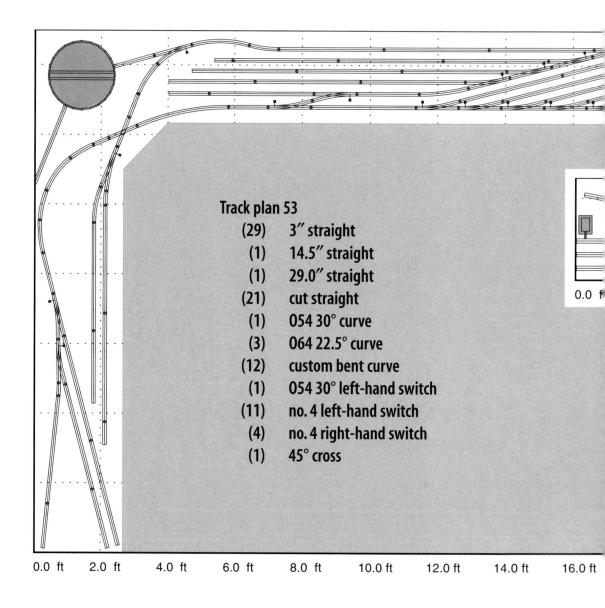

Track plan 53

(29)	3″ straight
(1)	14.5″ straight
(1)	29.0″ straight
(21)	cut straight
(1)	054 30° curve
(3)	064 22.5° curve
(12)	custom bent curve
(1)	054 30° left-hand switch
(11)	no. 4 left-hand switch
(4)	no. 4 right-hand switch
(1)	45° cross

0.0 f

0.0 ft   2.0 ft   4.0 ft   6.0 ft   8.0 ft   10.0 ft   12.0 ft   14.0 ft   16.0 ft

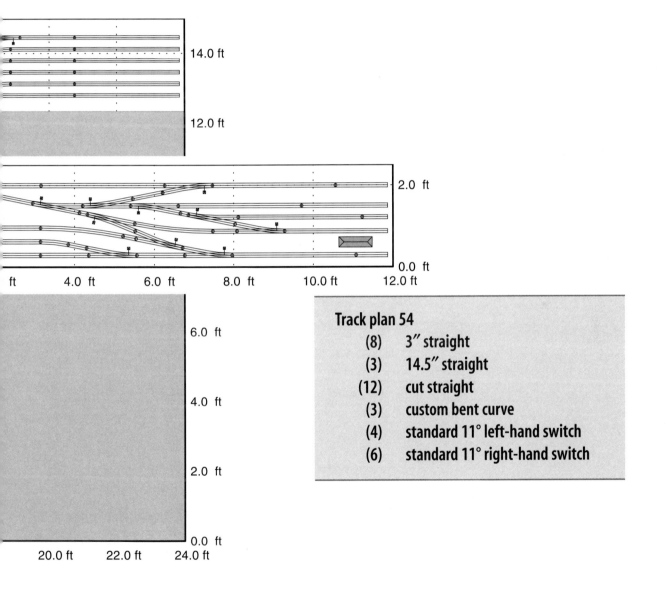

14.0 ft

12.0 ft

2.0 ft

0.0 ft

ft   4.0 ft   6.0 ft   8.0 ft   10.0 ft   12.0 ft

6.0 ft

4.0 ft

2.0 ft

0.0 ft

20.0 ft   22.0 ft   24.0 ft

Track plan 54

(8)	3″ straight
(3)	14.5″ straight
(12)	cut straight
(3)	custom bent curve
(4)	standard 11° left-hand switch
(6)	standard 11° right-hand switch

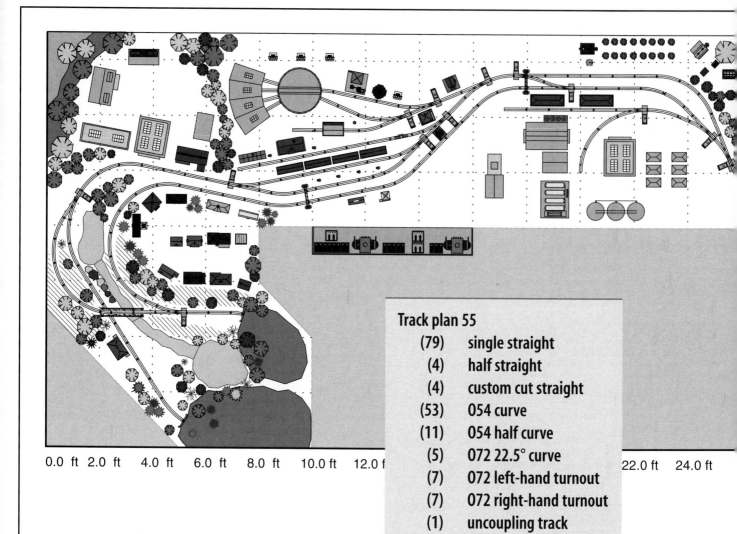

0.0 ft 2.0 ft 4.0 ft 6.0 ft 8.0 ft 10.0 ft 12.0 f... 22.0 ft 24.0 ft

Track plan 55

(79)	single straight
(4)	half straight
(4)	custom cut straight
(53)	054 curve
(11)	054 half curve
(5)	072 22.5° curve
(7)	072 left-hand turnout
(7)	072 right-hand turnout
(1)	uncoupling track

Track plan 56

(10)	3″ straight		(1)	063 45° curve
(1)	6.2″ straight		(2)	072 45° curve
(8)	12.4″ straight		(1)	080 30° curve
(17)	cut straight		(1)	0138 cut curve
(11)	032 45° curve		(3)	cut-to-radius curve
(4)	032 cut curve		(6)	042 left-hand turnout
(7)	042 45° curve		(10)	042 right-hand turnout
(1)	042 cut curve		(12)	042 makeup curve
(3)	054 45° curve		(1)	R-100 right-hand turnou...

14.0 ft

12.0 ft

10.0 ft

8.0 ft

6.0 ft

4.0 ft

2.0 ft

0.0 ft

.0 ft   30.0 ft   32.0 ft

20.0 ft

18.0 ft

16.0 ft

14.0 ft

12.0 ft

10.0 ft

8.0 ft

6.0 ft

4.0 ft

2.0 ft

0.0 ft

ft   2.0 ft   4.0 ft   6.0 ft   8.0 ft   10.0 ft   12.0 ft   14.0 ft   16.0 ft   18.0 ft   20.0 ft

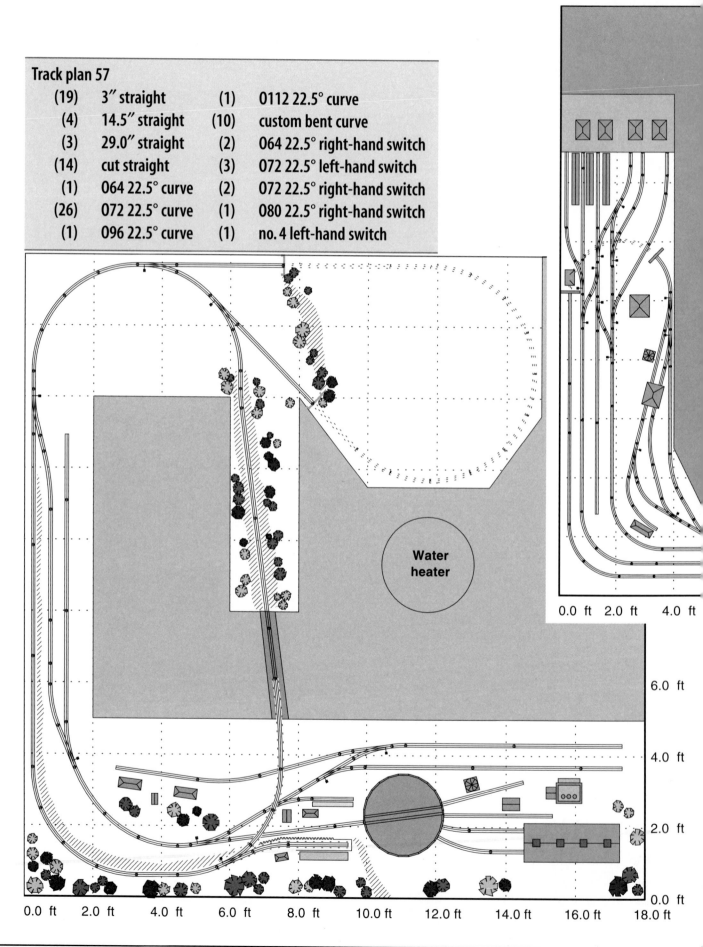

Track plan 57

(19)	3″ straight	(1)	0112 22.5° curve
(4)	14.5″ straight	(10)	custom bent curve
(3)	29.0″ straight	(2)	064 22.5° right-hand switch
(14)	cut straight	(3)	072 22.5° left-hand switch
(1)	064 22.5° curve	(2)	072 22.5° right-hand switch
(26)	072 22.5° curve	(1)	080 22.5° right-hand switch
(1)	096 22.5° curve	(1)	no. 4 left-hand switch

Water heater

0.0 ft 2.0 ft 4.0 ft

6.0 ft
4.0 ft
2.0 ft
0.0 ft

0.0 ft 2.0 ft 4.0 ft 6.0 ft 8.0 ft 10.0 ft 12.0 ft 14.0 ft 16.0 ft 18.0 ft

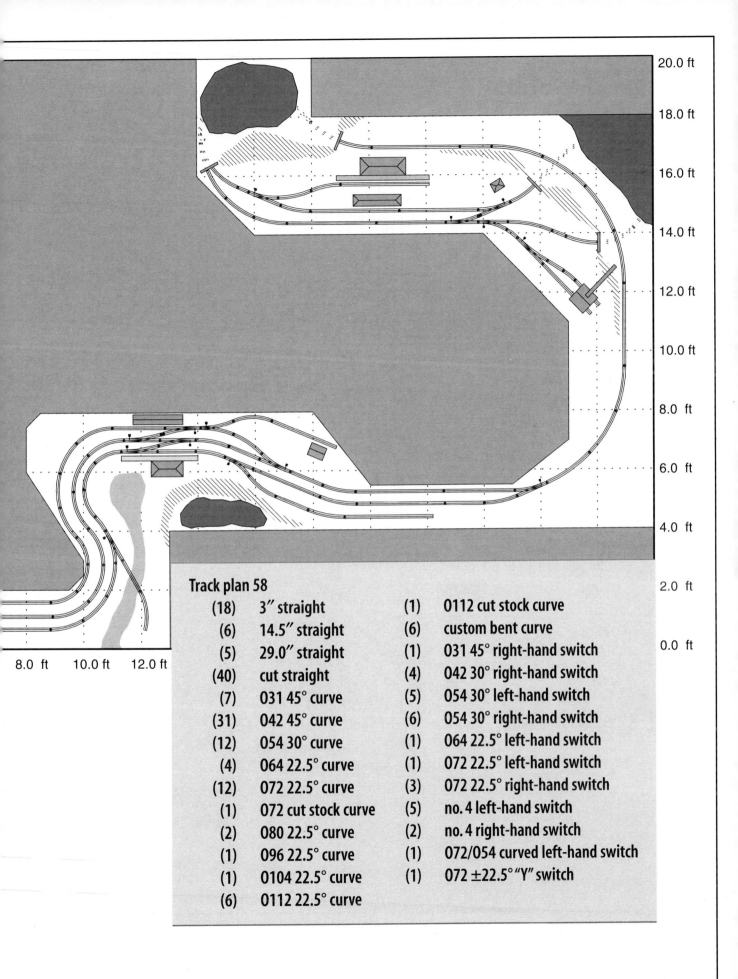

20.0 ft
18.0 ft
16.0 ft
14.0 ft
12.0 ft
10.0 ft
8.0 ft
6.0 ft
4.0 ft
2.0 ft
0.0 ft

8.0 ft   10.0 ft   12.0 ft

Track plan 58

(18)	3″ straight	(1)	0112 cut stock curve
(6)	14.5″ straight	(6)	custom bent curve
(5)	29.0″ straight	(1)	031 45° right-hand switch
(40)	cut straight	(4)	042 30° right-hand switch
(7)	031 45° curve	(5)	054 30° left-hand switch
(31)	042 45° curve	(6)	054 30° right-hand switch
(12)	054 30° curve	(1)	064 22.5° left-hand switch
(4)	064 22.5° curve	(1)	072 22.5° left-hand switch
(12)	072 22.5° curve	(3)	072 22.5° right-hand switch
(1)	072 cut stock curve	(5)	no. 4 left-hand switch
(2)	080 22.5° curve	(2)	no. 4 right-hand switch
(1)	096 22.5° curve	(1)	072/054 curved left-hand switch
(1)	0104 22.5° curve	(1)	072 ±22.5° "Y" switch
(6)	0112 22.5° curve		

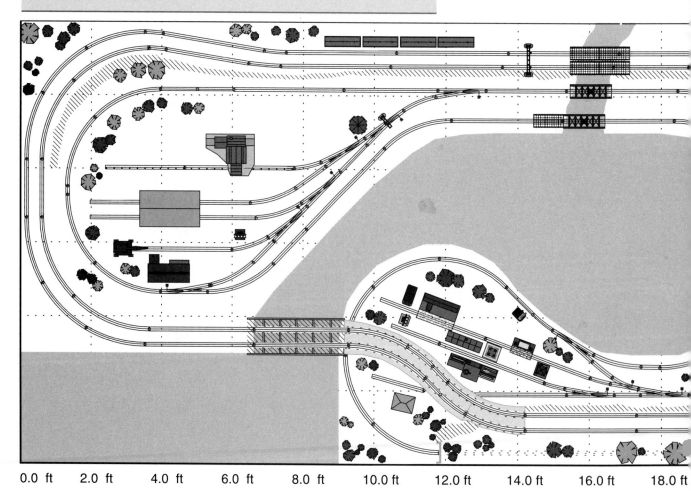

Track plan 59

(28)	3″ straight	(1)	072 cut curve
(2)	6.2″ straight	(14)	080 30° curve
(6)	12.4″ straight	(6)	080 cut curve
(2)	24.8″ straight	(3)	089 30° curve
(30)	cut straight	(1)	096 cut curve
(2)	042 cut curve	(1)	0138 cut curve
(1)	054 45° curve	(1)	cut-to-radius curve
(5)	054 cut curve	(1)	042 right-hand turnout
(13)	063 45° curve	(3)	R-100 left-hand turnout
(2)	063 cut curve	(7)	R-100 right-hand turnout
(14)	072 45° curve		

0.0 ft   2.0 ft   4.0 ft   6.0 ft   8.0 ft   10.0 ft   12.0 ft   14.0 ft   16.0 ft   18.0 ft

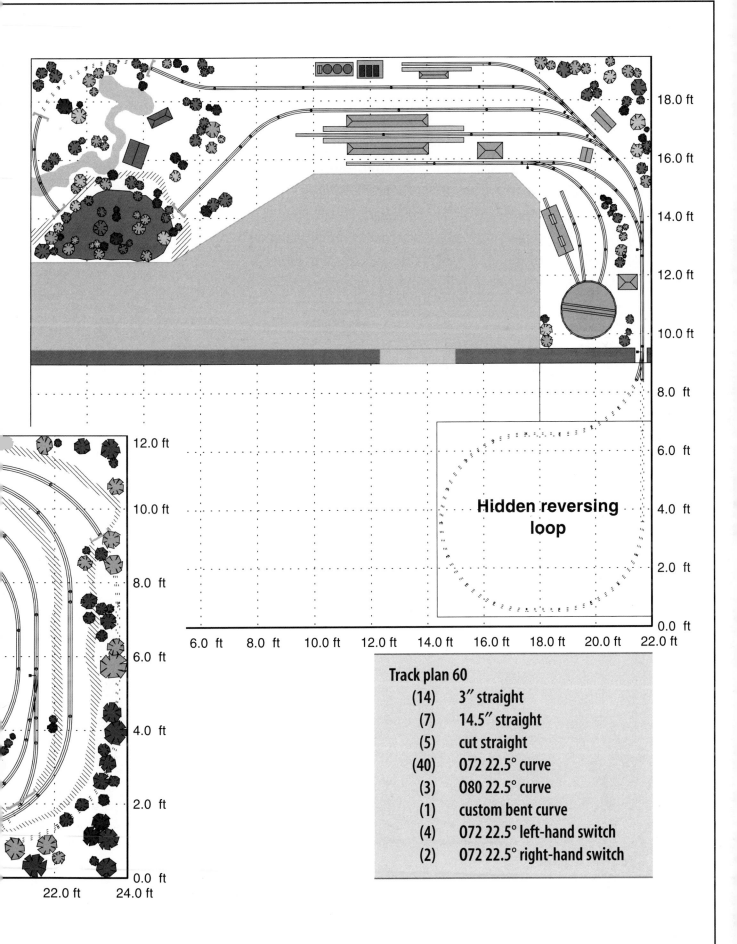

Hidden reversing loop

18.0 ft
16.0 ft
14.0 ft
12.0 ft
10.0 ft
8.0 ft
6.0 ft
4.0 ft
2.0 ft
0.0 ft

12.0 ft
10.0 ft
8.0 ft
6.0 ft
4.0 ft
2.0 ft
0.0 ft

6.0 ft   8.0 ft   10.0 ft   12.0 ft   14.0 ft   16.0 ft   18.0 ft   20.0 ft   22.0 ft

22.0 ft   24.0 ft

Track plan 60		
(14)	3″ straight
(7)	14.5″ straight
(5)	cut straight
(40)	072 22.5° curve
(3)	080 22.5° curve
(1)	custom bent curve
(4)	072 22.5° left-hand switch
(2)	072 22.5° right-hand switch

Track plan 61

(53)	3" straight	(1)	072 22.5° left-hand switch
(9)	14.5" straight	(2)	072 22.5° right-hand switch
(3)	29.0" straight	(1)	080 22.5° left-hand switch
(55)	cut straight	(1)	080 22.5° right-hand switch
(5)	054 30° curve	(1)	096 22.5° left-hand switch
(9)	064 22.5° curve	(12)	no. 4 left-hand switch
(31)	072 22.5° curve	(6)	no. 4 right-hand switch
(15)	080 22.5° curve	(2)	standard 11° left-hand switch
(13)	088 22.5° curve	(6)	standard 11° right-hand switch
(14)	096 22.5° curve	(6)	turnout transition curve
(23)	custom bent curve	(8)	no. 108 uncoupling track

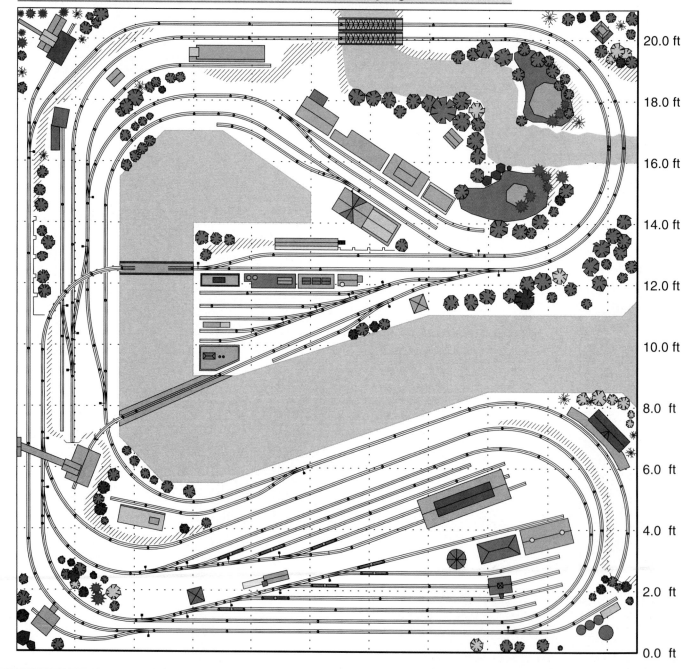

20.0 ft
18.0 ft
16.0 ft
14.0 ft
12.0 ft
10.0 ft
8.0 ft
6.0 ft
4.0 ft
2.0 ft
0.0 ft

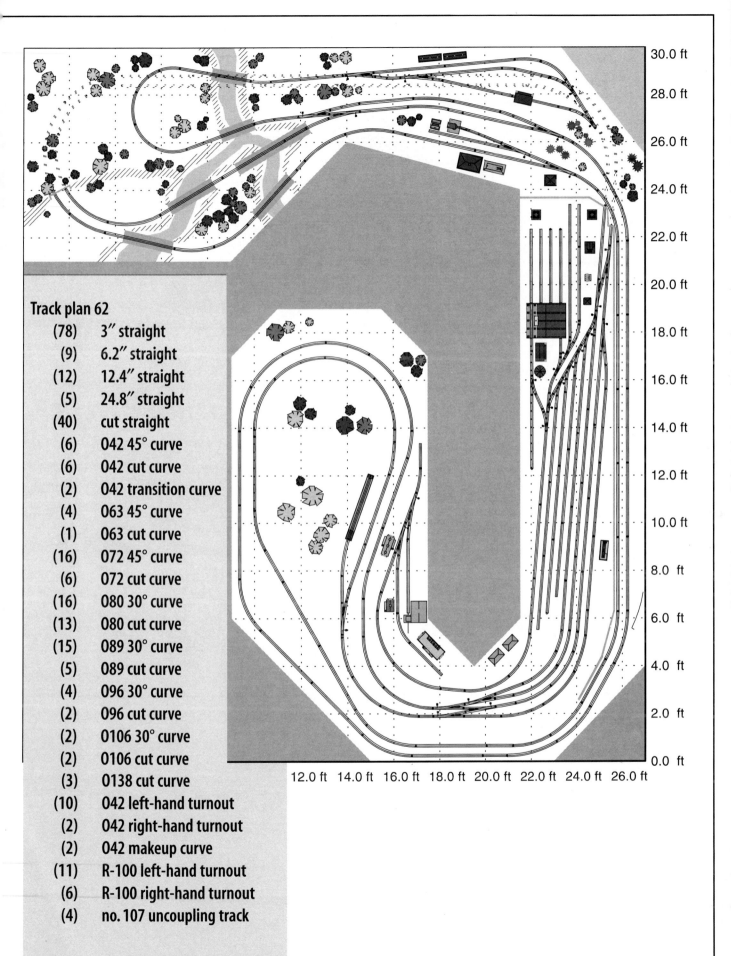

Track plan 62

(78)	3″ straight
(9)	6.2″ straight
(12)	12.4″ straight
(5)	24.8″ straight
(40)	cut straight
(6)	042 45° curve
(6)	042 cut curve
(2)	042 transition curve
(4)	063 45° curve
(1)	063 cut curve
(16)	072 45° curve
(6)	072 cut curve
(16)	080 30° curve
(13)	080 cut curve
(15)	089 30° curve
(5)	089 cut curve
(4)	096 30° curve
(2)	096 cut curve
(2)	0106 30° curve
(2)	0106 cut curve
(3)	0138 cut curve
(10)	042 left-hand turnout
(2)	042 right-hand turnout
(2)	042 makeup curve
(11)	R-100 left-hand turnout
(6)	R-100 right-hand turnout
(4)	no. 107 uncoupling track

30.0 ft
28.0 ft
26.0 ft
24.0 ft
22.0 ft
20.0 ft
18.0 ft
16.0 ft
14.0 ft
12.0 ft
10.0 ft
8.0 ft
6.0 ft
4.0 ft
2.0 ft
0.0 ft

12.0 ft   14.0 ft   16.0 ft   18.0 ft   20.0 ft   22.0 ft   24.0 ft   26.0 ft

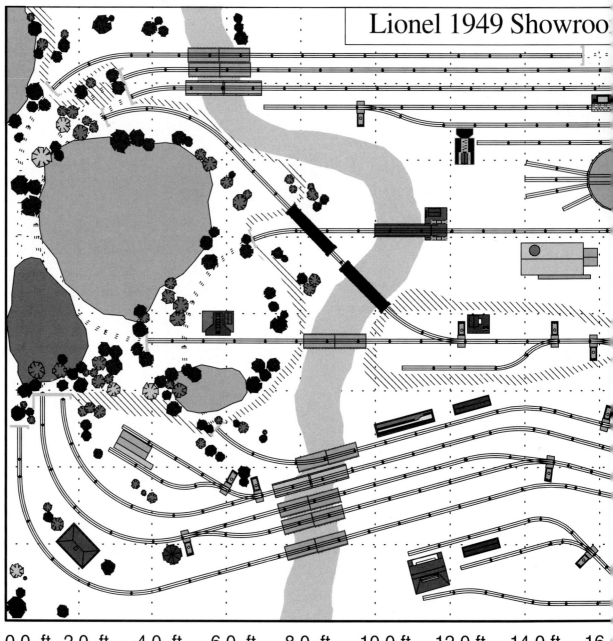

Lionel 1949 Showroo

0.0 ft 2.0 ft   4.0 ft   6.0 ft   8.0 ft   10.0 ft   12.0 ft   14.0 ft   16.

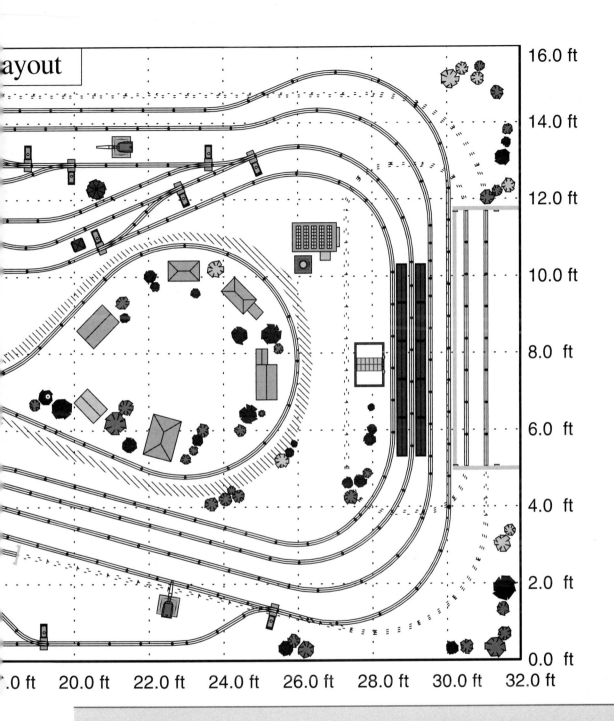

ayout

16.0 ft

14.0 ft

12.0 ft

10.0 ft

8.0 ft

6.0 ft

4.0 ft

2.0 ft

0.0 ft

.0 ft   20.0 ft   22.0 ft   24.0 ft   26.0 ft   28.0 ft   30.0 ft   32.0 ft

Track plan 63

(359)	single straight	(1)	054 cut curve
(24)	half straight	(109)	072 curve 22.5°
(13)	custom cut straight	(13)	072 cut curve
(11)	031 45° curve	(4)	031 left-hand turnout
(2)	031 cut curve	(3)	031 right-hand turnout
(8)	054 curve	(6)	072 left-hand turnout
(1)	054 half curve	(6)	072 right-hand turnout

SELECTED MANUFACTURERS AND SUPPLIERS

Atlas Model Railroad Co., Inc.
378 Florence Ave.
Hillside, NJ 07205
Locomotives, rolling stock, accessories, and track

Curtis High Rail Products, Inc.
P. O. Box 385
North Stonington, CT 06359
Track

GarGraves Trackage Corp.
8967 Ridge Rd.
North Rose, NY 14516-9793
Track

K-Line Electric Trains
P. O. Box 2831
Chapel Hill, NC 27515
Locomotives, rolling stock, accessories, and track

Lionel Corp.
50625 Richard W Blvd.
Chesterfield, MI 48051-2493
Locomotives, rolling stock, accessories, and track

MTH Electric Trains
9693-A Gerwig Lane
Columbia, MD 21046
Locomotives, rolling stock, accessories, and track

Ross Custom Switches
P. O. Box 110
North Stonington, CT 06359
Track and accessories

S-Helper Service, Inc.
2 Roberts Rd.
New Brunswick, NJ 08901-1621
Locomotives, rolling stock, and track